EXPLORING COUNTRIES

Ireland

by Colleen Sexton

BELLWETHER MEDIA • MINNEAPOLIS, MN

Note to Librarians, Teachers, and Parents:

Blastoff! Readers are carefully developed by literacy experts and combine standards-based content with developmentally appropriate text.

Level 1 provides the most support through repetition of high-frequency words, light text, predictable sentence patterns, and strong visual support.

Level 2 offers early readers a bit more challenge through varied simple sentences, increased text load, and less repetition of high-frequency words.

Level 3 advances early-fluent readers toward fluency through increased text and concept load, less reliance on visuals, longer sentences, and more literary language.

Level 4 builds reading stamina by providing more text per page, increased use of punctuation, greater variation in sentence patterns, and increasingly challenging vocabulary.

Level 5 encourages children to move from "learning to read" to "reading to learn" by providing even more text, varied writing styles, and less familiar topics.

Whichever book is right for your reader, Blastoff! Readers are the perfect books to build confidence and encourage a love of reading that will last a lifetime!

This edition first published in 2011 by Bellwether Media, Inc.

No part of this publication may be reproduced in whole or in part without written permission of the publisher. For information regarding permission, write to Bellwether Media, Inc., Attention: Permissions Department, 5357 Penn Avenue South, Minneapolis, MN 55419.

Library of Congress Cataloging-in-Publication Data

Sexton, Colleen A., 1967-
Ireland / by Colleen Sexton.
   p. cm. – (Exploring countries) (Blastoff! Readers)
Includes bibliographical references and index.
Summary: "Developed by literacy experts for students in grades three through seven, this book introduces young readers to the geography and culture of Ireland"–Provided by publisher.
ISBN 978-1-60014-483-7 (hardcover : alk. paper)
1. Ireland–Juvenile literature. I. Title.
DA906.S49 2011
941.5–dc22   2010015687

Printed in the United States of America, North Mankato, MN.

080110   1162

Contents

Scotland

Atlantic Ocean

Northern
Ireland

Irish Sea

Dublin ★

Ireland

Wales

Ireland is a small country in northwestern Europe, covering
an area of 27,133 square miles (70,273 square kilometers).
It shares the island of Ireland with Northern Ireland, a part
of the **United Kingdom**. England, Wales, and Scotland
lie to the east across the Irish Sea. They make up the rest
of the United Kingdom.

England

fun fact
No place in Ireland is more than 70 miles (113 kilometers) from the ocean!

The Atlantic Ocean splashes against Ireland's northern, southern, and western shores. Hundreds of small islands off the western coast belong to Ireland. Dublin is the country's capital and largest city.

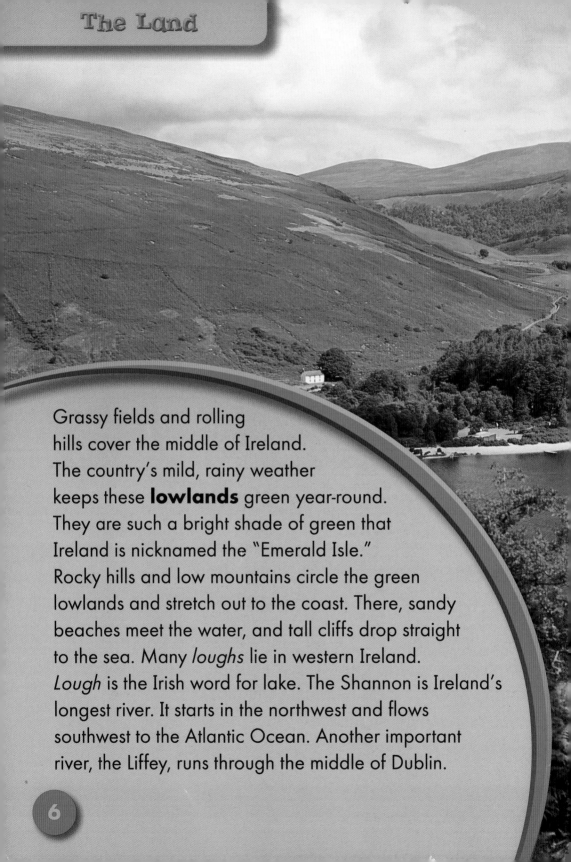

Grassy fields and rolling hills cover the middle of Ireland. The country's mild, rainy weather keeps these **lowlands** green year-round. They are such a bright shade of green that Ireland is nicknamed the "Emerald Isle." Rocky hills and low mountains circle the green lowlands and stretch out to the coast. There, sandy beaches meet the water, and tall cliffs drop straight to the sea. Many *loughs* lie in western Ireland. *Lough* is the Irish word for lake. The Shannon is Ireland's longest river. It starts in the northwest and flows southwest to the Atlantic Ocean. Another important river, the Liffey, runs through the middle of Dublin.

fun fact

Over hundreds of years, many different people have built castles throughout Ireland. Today, the ruins of around 3,000 castles dot Ireland's many landscapes.

peat

fun fact

Mummies have been found in Ireland's bogs! The bog water preserved the bodies of people who died hundreds of years ago. Many of the mummies still have skin, hair, and even clothes.

Bogs cover many parts of Ireland. These wet, spongy areas of land often began as lakes. Plants there grew, died, and started to rot. This plant material formed a thick mat called **peat**, which soon filled the lakes. The Irish have used peat as fuel for hundreds of years. They dig it up, dry it out, and burn it in their fireplaces. Some power plants also burn peat to produce energy. Today, some Irish are working to protect the bogs. They believe people are digging up too much peat. The bogs could soon disappear as they have in other European countries.

Connemara ponies

fun fact

Long ago, Connemara ponies ran wild in western Ireland. Farmers tamed them and now this strong, gentle breed is a top sporting horse. It is one of the best show jumpers in the world!

The Irish have a deep respect for the many animals and plants that share their home. Fields and bogs provide shelter for small animals like rabbits, foxes, and badgers. Salmon, pike, trout, and other fish swim in Ireland's lakes and rivers. Seals and otters live along the rocky coasts. Bird-watchers can spot puffins, herons, ospreys, and more than 400 other kinds of birds.

puffin

shamrock

fox

Ireland also has many unique plants. The flowers of the Irish orchid and the Kerry lily decorate Ireland's countryside. The butterwort plant traps and eats bugs. The most famous Irish plant is the shamrock. This three-leafed plant is a **symbol** of Ireland.

Ireland is home to over 4 million people. Most are Irish. Their **ancestors** came to the island long ago from different parts of Europe. The Irish developed their own **traditions** and way of life. They spoke **Gaelic**. This language has survived in Ireland for more than 2,000 years.

Did you know?

English and Irish are the official languages of Ireland. Street signs often appear in both languages.

Speak Irish!

English	Irish	How to say it
hello	dia ḍuit	JEE-uh dich
good-bye	slán	SLAWN
yes	ja	YAH
no	nej	NAY
please	más é do thoil é	maw-shay-duh-HULL-ay
thank you	go raibh maith agat	guh-ruh-MAH-huh-guht
friend	cara	KAW-rah

! fun fact

Many Irish do not use "yes" or "no" to answer questions. If someone asked them if they were lucky, they would say, "I am" or "I am not."

In 1169, England attacked Ireland and ruled it for more than 750 years. The English rented small plots of land to the Irish, who grew potatoes. This crop was their main source of food. In the 1840s, the crop failed. About one million Irish died of starvation. Many more left the country in the years that followed. In the late 1900s, new job opportunities brought many Irish back. Today, **immigrants** come to Ireland from all over the world.

13

Most Irish live in large towns or cities. Dublin, Cork, Galway, Limerick, and Waterford are busy cities with shops, offices, and factories. People live in apartments or in small houses with yards. Trains and buses take them around their cities and across the country.

Where People Live in Ireland

countryside 39%

cities 61%

In the countryside, people live in small, traditional cottages or modern homes. They grow crops or raise sheep and cows on the green fields. Each neighborhood has at least one **public house**, or pub, where neighbors gather to chat and listen to music. Most towns also have at least one church. Many Irish are **Catholic** and go to church regularly.

The Catholic Church runs most of Ireland's schools.
Girls and boys often go to separate schools.
Most wear uniforms to school every day.

Students start classes by the time they are 6 years old. They study reading, writing, math, and science. They learn traditional dances and go on outdoor adventures in gym class. Students also study Irish. At age 17, students take tests to get into one of Ireland's universities.

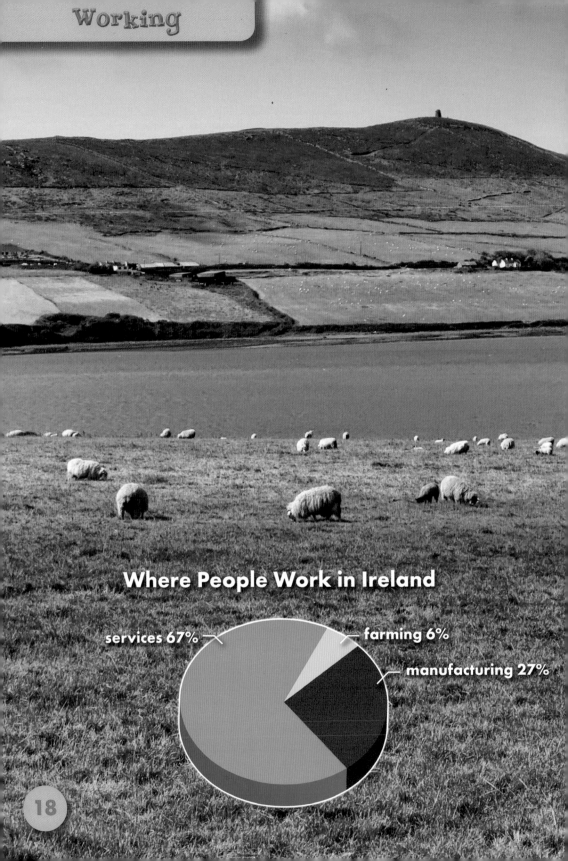

Where People Work in Ireland

services 67%

farming 6%

manufacturing 27%

For hundreds of years, most Irish made a living as farmers. Today, there are fewer farmers, but they have larger farms than their ancestors. They grow barley, oats, and potatoes. Many raise hogs, sheep, and cattle.

In cities, more than half of all Irish hold **service jobs**. They work in banks, schools, and hospitals. Many people have jobs in hotels, restaurants, and shops that serve the millions of visitors who come to Ireland each year. Irish factory workers make food products, medicine, **textiles**, and computers. These goods are shipped from Ireland's ports to countries around the world.

rugby

The Irish enjoy many activities in their free time. They listen to music, watch TV, and stroll to the pub for some *craic*. That's the Irish word for fun! Sailing, fishing, and golf are common activities. Many Irish cheer for their national soccer and rugby teams.

Fans come out for Gaelic football too. This Irish sport has rules from both soccer and rugby. **Hurling** is another popular Gaelic sport. It is at least 1,000 years old and is still played today. In this fast-moving game, players try to hit a ball into a goal with axe-shaped sticks.

hurling

fun fact

On average, an Irish person eats 266 bowls of breakfast cereal per year.

Irish families come together at mealtime. Oatmeal, baked beans on toast, and potato pancakes called *boxty* are often served for breakfast. Other morning favorites include bacon, eggs, and fried tomatoes. Tea is a favorite drink enjoyed with soda bread or scones. Many traditional dishes use potatoes. Irish stew is a mix of potatoes, onions, and mutton, or meat from sheep. *Colcannon* combines potatoes and cabbage. *Coddle* is a national dish. It is made from bacon, sausage, and potatoes. Fish soup and fish pie feature halibut, herring, or cod caught from the surrounding sea.

Irish stew

Did you know?
Many of Ireland's dairy farmers are also cheese makers. Irish cheeses such as Cashel Blue, Gubbeen, and Dubliner are famous around the world for their flavor.

colcannon

Many holidays in Ireland are religious. Families gather to celebrate Christmas and Easter. On Saint Brigid's Day in February, people hang straw crosses from their doorways for good luck. On All Souls' Day in November, many Irish visit the graves of family members who have died.

Saint Patrick's Day is March 17. This is Ireland's national holiday. The Irish pin shamrocks to their clothes. They go to church and gather with friends and family for a special meal. Parades wind down the streets of many towns and cities.

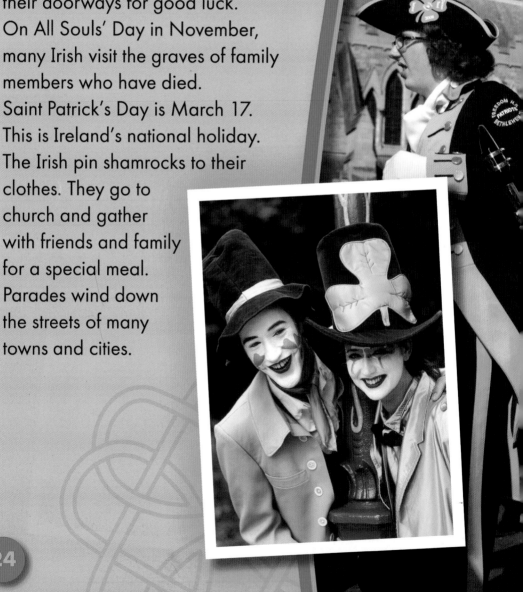

fun fact

Communities throughout Ireland have *céilís*. These big parties feature food, music, dancing, and storytelling.

! fun fact

Irish musicians have played the harp for at least 1,000 years. It is Ireland's official national symbol.

The arts are an important part of Irish life. Ireland has a long tradition of storytelling. Tales of ghosts, giants, fairies, and **leprechauns** have been passed down through time. Singers also tell stories. Irish **ballads** are often sad tales about Ireland's history. A lone singer without instruments sings old songs, or *sean-nós*.

Musicians pick up fiddles, wooden flutes, **accordions**, harps, and banjos to play dancing music. Drummers keep time on *bodhráns*. People take to the dance floor to try reels and jigs. Step dancers hold their upper bodies still as their feet step and kick with great speed. The arts are a way to celebrate the story of Ireland!

Did you know?

Patterns of curving lines, spirals, and knots adorn traditional Irish paintings, stone carvings, clothing, and jewelry.

Fast Facts About Ireland

Ireland's Flag

Ireland's flag has three vertical stripes. The green stripe stands for the Irish Catholic people. The orange stands for the English Protestant people who once ruled Ireland. The white stripe in the middle stands for peace between these groups. This flag was first raised in 1916 in Dublin. The country adopted it in 1919.

Official Name: Ireland

Area: 27,133 square miles (70,273 square kilometers); Ireland is the 119th largest country in the world.

Capital City:	Dublin
Important Cities:	Cork, Galway, Limerick, Waterford
Population:	4,250,163 (July 2010)
Official Languages:	English and Irish
National Holiday:	Saint Patrick's Day (March 17)
Religions:	Christian (92.2%), Other (7.8%)
Major Industries:	farming, fishing, manufacturing, mining, services, tourism
Natural Resources:	farmland, natural gas, peat, copper, lead, zinc, limestone
Manufactured Products:	food products, clothing, medicine, chemicals, machinery, glass and crystal, computer products
Farm Products:	potatoes, turnips, barley, sugar beets, wheat, oats, beef, dairy products
Unit of Money:	euro; the euro is divided into 100 cents.

Glossary

accordions—box-shaped instruments; an accordion has a keyboard on one side, buttons to make low sounds on the other side, and a part called a bellows in the middle.

ancestors—relatives who lived long ago

ballads—songs that tell stories

bogs—areas of wet, spongy ground

Catholic—members of the Roman Catholic Church; Roman Catholics are Christian.

Gaelic—an ancient language brought to Ireland by the Celts long ago; many Gaelic traditions, such as sports and music, are part of Irish culture today.

hurling—a fast-moving game similar to field hockey that is played with axe-shaped sticks and a small ball

immigrants—people who leave one country to live in another country

leprechauns—elves in Irish folktales who will reveal a hidden treasure if caught

lowlands—areas of land that are lower than the surrounding land

peat—plant material soaked with water that builds up over time; dried peat is used as fuel.

public house—a neighborhood gathering place that serves food and drinks; public houses are also called pubs.

service jobs—jobs that perform tasks for people or businesses

symbol—something that stands for something else; the harp and shamrock are symbols of Ireland.

textiles—fabrics or clothes that have been woven or knitted

traditions—stories, beliefs, or ways of life that families or groups hand down from one generation to another

United Kingdom—a state that includes England, Scotland, Wales, and Northern Ireland

To Learn More

AT THE LIBRARY
Doyle, Malachy. *Tales from Old Ireland*.
Cambridge, Mass.: Barefoot Books, 2006.

Koponen, Libby. *Ireland*. New York, N.Y.: Children's
Press, 2009.

Sasek, Miroslav. *This Is Ireland*. New York, N.Y.:
Universe Publishing, 2005.

ON THE WEB
Learning more about Ireland
is as easy as 1, 2, 3.

1. Go to www.factsurfer.com.

2. Enter "Ireland" into the search box.

3. Click the "Surf" button and you will see a list of
   related Web sites.

With factsurfer.com, finding more information is just
a click away.

Index

The images in this book are reproduced through the courtesy of: John Blake, front cover; Maisei Raman, front cover (flag), p. 28; Juan Eppardo, pp. 4-5; The Irish Image Collection/Photolibrary, pp. 6-7, 14, 15, 19 (top), 24 (small); Juan Martinez, pp. 7 (small), 11 (top & middle), 16, 18, 29 (bill & coin); Thierry Maffeis, pp. 8-9; Robin Bush/Photolibrary, p. 9 (small); Juniors Bildarchiv/Photolibrary, pp. 10-11; Paul Morton, p. 11 (bottom); Jacque Denzer Parker/Photolibrary, p. 13; Keith Levit Photography/Photolibrary, p. 17; Ikonography Collection/Alamy, p. 19 (bottom); Getty Images, p. 20; Joe Fox/Alamy, p. 21; Comstock/Photolibrary, p. 22; Monkey Business Images, p. 23 (top & bottom); Striking Images/Alamy, pp. 24-25; Alistair Dove/Alamy, p. 26; Chris Cooper-Smith/Alamy, p. 27.